Giving is a facet of a larger subject called stewardship. According to James 1:17, God owns everything because He is the Creator, Maker and Giver of all things — so when we give, we are merely giving back a portion of what belongs to God anyway. Our stewardship towards God includes everything that we have been given and how we use this on behalf of the Lord and for the Lord's work. We are stewards of the abilities, spiritual gifts, knowledge, money, in fact, everything that we have been given — but today we focus only on the Biblical principles of giving. This giving is only one facet of our stewardship.

Five Basic Principles

There are five basic principles of Biblical giving.

Giving is a measure of one's love for God: Matthew 6:19-21 teaches that the believer should lay up treasures in heaven, for where one's treasure is, there your heart is also. If we lay up treasures in heaven, our heart will be on heavenly things. Further, 1 Timothy 6:17-18 teaches that the rich should have their hope set on God and be ready to give out of their wealth. Believers must remember our hope is not on wealth, but on the Lord God (cf. Titus 2:11-14). According to 1 John 3:17, if one does not give, then the question is, "Does the love of God abide in that person?"

Giving as an expression of one's faith: James 2:15-17 teaches that the believer's faith becomes useful when it is expressed through works. The work of giving therefore shows one's faith. The believer is not saved by works, but shows his or her faith through their works.

Giving more results in receiving more: This is not a license for the name-it-and-grab-it movement, but simply to say that the believer can never out-give God. This is a promise from God: Give and it shall be given unto you (Luke 6:38). Further, Philippians 4:15-19 teaches that God will supply the believer's needs (not 'wants').

Giving should be done in secret: Matthew 6:1-4 states that giving should be done in secret, not for show. Keep your giving between you and God.

Giving produces a willingness to work: The believer should be willing to work in order to be able to give more (cf. Acts 20:33-35).

Principles Found in 2 Corinthians 8:1-15

Paul deals with eight points relating to giving in 2 Corinthians 8:1-15. First, poverty is not an excuse not to give. Look at the Macedonians: out of their poverty they still practised grace giving (2 Cor 8:1-2). Second, giving is an opportunity to be sought and chased after! (2 Cor 8:3-4).

Third, give yourself first to the Lord (2 Cor 8:5). Fourth, giving is proof of your love of God (2 Cor 8:6-8). Fifth, Christ is the example of a great giver (2 Cor 8:9). Sixth, be willing to make a pledge and more willing to fulfil it if God provides (2 Cor 8:10-11). Seventh, give willingly (2 Cor 8:12). Our willingness makes it acceptable to God. However, if we give grudgingly, it may help the one who receives it, but it does not put the giver in good standing before the Lord. It is better not to give than to give grudgingly. Eighth, do not give to the point of poverty but to the point of equality (2 Cor 8:13-15).

Principles Found in 2 Corinthians 9:6-14

Paul provides seven principles relating to giving in this passage. First, what you sow you will reap (2 Cor 9:6). If you sow bountifully, you will reap bountifully (but the inverse is also true: if you sow sparingly…). Second, give as you purposed in your heart to give, but not grudgingly (2 Cor 9:7a). Third, God loves a cheerful giver (2 Cor 9:7b). Giving should be done with a cheerful attitude, even hilariously (the Greek word means "hilarious"). Fourth, God will supply the giver's needs (2 Cor 9:8-11). Fifth, giving is a form of worship of God (2 Cor 9:12). Sixth, a believer's giving is proof of one's love for God and it brings glory to God (2 Cor 9:13). Seventh, giving is a form of fellowship with other believers who are not present (2 Cor 9:14).

Thanks be to God for his unspeakable gift (2 Cor 9:15). What is God's unspeakable gift? The gift that God gave was His own Son, who became poor so that believers might become spiritually rich. That is the greatest gift that God can provide. God provided salvation, but it cost Him something; it cost Him the life of His Son. The giving of believers may cost us something, but just as God's sending His Son was a measure of His love for the world (John 3:16), so the believer should be proving his or her love for God by giving as well.

18 Scriptures On Giving You Can Share Before Your Next Offering Time

Giving is always seem to struggle with. For many pastors, it can be hard to even talk about it in church services.

However, it's important to inspire your people with what God says about giving. There are hundreds of scriptures on giving to help you encourage members to be generous with their finances.

Before your next offering time, start by sharing one of these scriptures to get your church family to start thinking about giving. You might be surprised at just how effective this is for your church.

The Bible Says To Give

As a pastor or church leader, you already know what the Bible says about giving. In fact, you could probably quote multiple scriptures right now that talk about giving. However, you probably don't talk about those scriptures that often.

Part of your responsibility as a pastor is to help explain the Bible to your members. This includes helping them understand what the Bible says about giving and why it's so important. Some great scriptures on giving to share with your members and online followers include:

Each of you should give what you have decided in your heart to give, not reluctantly or under compulsion, for God loves a cheerful giver. – 2 Corinthians 9:7

This one is incredibly important for explaining that you should give what you can and want.

For if the willingness is there, the gift is acceptable according to what one has, not according to what one does not have. – 2 Corinthians 8:12

Yet another example the Bible provides about giving what you can and that that is enough.

"Bring the whole tithe into the storehouse, that there may be food in my house. Test me in this," says the Lord Almighty, "and see if I will not throw open the floodgates of heaven and pour out so much blessing that there will not be room enough to store it." – Malachi 3:10

Ideal for explaining that giving leads to more blessings in life.

All day long he craves for more, but the righteous give without sparing. – Proverbs 21:26

Explains that giving is more important than wanting more than what one needs.

You will be enriched in every way so that you can be generous on every occasion, and through your generosity will result in thanksgiving to God. – 2 Corinthians 9:11

Another example of giving in which generosity is rewarded.

A gift opens the way and ushers the giver into the presence of the great. – Proverbs 18:16

To open oneself to greatness, they must first give.

Give, and it will be given to you. A good measure, pressed down, shaken together and running over, will be poured into your lap. For with the measure you use, it will be measured to you. – Luke 6:38

It's important to give in order to receive great things in return.

Now he who supplies seed to the sower and bread for food will also supply and increase your store of seed and will enlarge the harvest of your righteousness. – 2 Corinthians 9:10

Giving to others doesn't just benefit the recipient, but the giver as well.

And he blessed him and said, "Blessed be Abram by God Most High, Possessor of heaven and earth; and blessed be God Most High, who has delivered your enemies into your hand!"And Abram gave him a tenth of everything. – Genesis 14:19–20

Helps explain where the idea of 10% of one's income came from.

All who were willing, men and women alike, came and brought gold jewelry of all kinds: brooches, earrings, rings ornaments. They all presented their gold as a wave offering to the Lord. – Exodus 35:22

Showcases the purpose of giving as a way to honor God.

A tithe of everything from the land, whether grain from the soil or fruit from the trees, belongs to the Lord; it is holy to the Lord. – Leviticus 27:30

Explains that God gave blessings to you and as such, people should give back to God to say thank you.

God's people faithfully brought in the contributions, tithes and dedicated gifts. – 2 Chronicles 31:12

Shows that giving is about more than just money, but that all contributions are important.

The people continued to bring freewill offerings morning after morning. So all the skilled craftsmen who were doing all the work on the sanctuary left their work and said to Moses, "The people are bringing more than enough for doing the work the LORD commanded to be done." Then Moses gave an order…"No man or woman is to make anything else as an offering for the sanctuary." And so the people were restrained from bringing more. – Exodus 36:3–6

Helps explain to your members that giving is what helps the and grow.

As for the rich in this present age, charge them not to be haughty, nor to set their hopes on the uncertainty of riches, but on God, who richly provides us with everything to enjoy. They are to do good, to be rich in good works, to be generous and ready to share, thus storing up treasure for themselves as a good foundation for the future, so that they may take hold of that which is truly life. – 1 Timothy 6:17-19

This helps to explain that you should give back to God in thanks so that you may enjoy the benefits of your generosity later in life.

Sell your possessions, and give to the needy. Provide yourselves with moneybags that do not grow old, with a treasure in the heavens that does not fail, where no thief approaches and no moth destroys. For where your treasure is, there will your heart be also. – Luke 12:33-34

Reminds members of how good it makes one feel to give selflessly to help those who are in need.

Whoever is generous to the poor lends to the Lord, and he will repay him for his deed. – Proverbs 19:17

Giving to others is like giving to God and that generosity is always favored.

One gives freely, yet grows all the richer; another withholds what he should give, and only suffers want. Whoever brings blessing will be enriched, and one who waters will himself be watered. – Proverbs 11:24-25

It's always important to give because making others happy is a type of wealth that surpasses financial riches.

Do not neglect to do good and to share what you have, for such sacrifices are pleasing to God. – Hebrews 13:16

Reminds members that God is happy when they share what they have to help others.

Why Aren't People Giving

To make sure you pick the right scriptures on giving, it's important to understand people sometimes struggle to give. The reasons vary greatly and it's a good idea to do an anonymous poll to see what the reasons are for your church.

If you have an online tithing option, which you should definitely consider, place the poll online too to help you better understand your online church family. The more you understand the reasons, the easier it is to work on the root cause of the challenges.

Online giving provider Tithe.ly discovered many members don't tithe anymore and also explored the reasons including:

Trouble with their beliefs – This is often the case with new members and those experiencing hard times after a major loss or change in their lives.

They're just trying out your church in their search to find a new church home.

They don't understand the reason your church needs them to give.

Finances are a struggle at the time, which isn't all that uncommon for many families who barely make it from paycheck to paycheck.

They're uncertain why God wants them to tithe.

They don't carry cash and aren't sure how else to give.

Of course, some just don't believe in tithing at all. Luckily, scriptures on giving are helpful in most of these cases.

Giving, Just Not To The Church

One other thing to consider is that your members may be giving, but just not to your church. Or, they split giving between their church and charities they believe in. Many Christian leaders are okay with this, as long as the church still has enough funds to run.

Before you feel like faith isn't important to your members, know that faith-based giving is still the top area where people give. This means faith is still a priority, but they want to help support charities and other non-profits as well to help make the world a better place.

In fact, a Lifeway study found that 83% of church goers believe tithing is important. Most believe that it's okay to split their giving between other Christian charities, including giving to other churches. However, 18% believe secular charities count as part of their regular tithing.

Explaining Why Tithing Is Important

If you want your members to give, you have to explain to them why it's important. Simply saying "the Bible says so" isn't enough. It's also not enough to just pass a collection plate around or have a link on your church's website saying "please give."

Think of your church as a business. Before anyone buys something (in this case, buying would be tithing), they want to know why they should. While you don't have to provide complete transparency, you need to explain not only the biblical reasons why giving is so important, but the financial reasons.

How much do your members know about how their donations are used? How much do they know about your church's financial needs? Odds are, they don't have a clue about either. They also probably don't have any idea about how much is used for local and global community work.

Before you start sharing scriptures on giving, create an area on your website explaining the following:

A breakdown of how church donations are allocated by percentage

The costs of running the church, including your average power bill and average salaries (these can all be lumped together)

The costs of marketing and outreach programs

Charities and local organizations your church is affiliated with

Cost of ministering outside of the church

Percentage used to help with the local community

Percentage used to aid in global endeavors

All of that might seem like it's best left with your church's accountant, this type of transparency makes it easier for your members to fully understand what type of financial needs your church has.

Along with posting this on your website, offer pamphlets to your members so they can look over the numbers, even if they don't go online. This is especially important if your church doesn't have a website yet.

While this is just a handful of scriptures on giving, it provides you with a start to share with your members. Of course, now that you have some examples of what to share, it's time to figure out the best ways to share them before your next offering.

Sharing More About Giving

While you can add giving scriptures to your sermons, you're not just limited to that time. In fact, it's a good idea to share these scriptures throughout the week. Sharing outside of church helps keep thoughts about giving alive all week long.

While a member might not give on Sunday, they might see your shared scripture and choose to give online to your church on a Thursday instead. Remember, the idea is to increase tithing not just during church, but every single day.

Start by choosing a scripture to share for the week. It's best to pick just one or two to avoid sounding greedy. You want to guide and inspire instead.

Once you have your scriptures, share them on your social media pages. Use them as the basis for a blog post. Send them out as a text. You could also have a daily scripture that you share in a newsletter, on your website or via social media.

If you do daily or weekly Bible studies online, through email or via text, add a scripture on giving once in a while. Sharing these regularly will help better explain the importance of giving to the church and all those in need. Once you've inspired regular giving in just one person, they'll help inspire others as well.

7 Biblical Benefits of Giving

Whenever there's a crisis that causes a drastic downfall in our economy, is it really wise—or required of us—to give? Certainly, God knows when we don't have much money and He wants us to be wise with what we have, right? Besides, if God owns it all...why does He need our money?

The answer is He doesn't. We don't give out of God's need for anything. We give out of ours.

While on this earth, Jesus talked more about money than hell.

That tells us it's an issue that's pretty important to Him. But not because He cares about or has need of money. He knows how important it tends to be to us. Jesus said the greatest commandment was to love God with all one's heart, soul, and mind (Matthew 22:37). That means with our money, too, especially if it owns (or occupies) much of our hearts.

There are many teachings in Scripture to give sacrificially—not just of our time and abilities, but of our money, too. And in the middle of crises everywhere might be the best time of all to consider giving more. Of all the reasons Scripture gives us to part with what's closest to our hearts, here are just seven biblical reasons to give—especially now:

1. Giving Is Evidence of Our Obedience to God

The church reformer Martin Luther believed every Christian needed two conversions: one for his soul and one for his pocketbook.

Anybody can say "I believe in God" and even "I'll follow You, Jesus." But when we give, as Scripture instructs, and it's sacrificial (give until it hurts) then our heart is involved. That's an obedient follower...one who is willing to put his money where his mouth is.

How is giving an act of obedience?

In the Old Testament Law, God told the Israelites to give a tenth of what they owned to the Lord for the support of the priesthood. Under the New Covenant, Jesus instructed His followers to give generously in proportion to how we would like God to be generous toward us (Luke 6:38).

He also wants us to give out of a grateful response to what we've been given. When we've been given salvation, haven't we been given everything? In that regard, Jesus didn't teach us to give just a tenth…He taught us, in some ways, to give our all.

Giving our all to Jesus—of our time, talents and treasure—is evidence of not just our obedience, but our love for Him.

2. Giving Sets Our Priorities Straight

Look at where you spend your money and you'll see where your heart is. We invest not just our time, but our money, in what is most important to us.

Is it your expensive home or its elaborate furnishings? Is it your children and their many activities? Is it that ring on your spouse's finger, or your luxury car, or high-tech toys and devices to impress others? Jesus told His followers to "store up for yourselves treasures in heaven, where neither moth nor rust destroys, and where thieves do not break in or steal; for where your treasure is, there your heart will be also" (Matthew 6:20-21).

That is our command to invest in the eternal. God's Word also tells us to be heavenly minded by setting our minds "on things above" (Colossians 3:2). If our priority is in the eternal and our sights are set on the life to come, that's where our money will be directed—to benefit the kingdom of God.

Therefore, as we give to God and invest in His kingdom, that's where our hearts will be fixed and focused. Giving to God prioritizes our lives and is, again, evidence of our love for Him.

3. Giving Increases Our Faith

Giving is not about how much money you have, it's about how much faith you have.

How much do you trust God that if you give obediently, He'll provide for all that you need? My husband and I (who have lived on a small-church pastor's salary most of our lives) have discovered through the years that when we are obedient to faithfully give from the first of what we receive each month, God is always faithful in providing all we need. It's when we don't give, that we end up lacking.

Giving is clearly a matter of trust. The more you give, the more you learn to trust God that you will have enough left over for your own needs. And the more you trust, the more you'll give. Again, put your money where your mouth is when you say "I trust God" and put Him to the test.

God takes that trust issue so seriously that the issue of money is the only area in which God tells us to test Him. Elsewhere Scripture says do not test the Lord your God (Deuteronomy 6:16, Luke 4:12, Acts 15:10).

Yet, in Malachi 3:10, God said, "Bring the whole tithe into the storehouse, so that there may be food in My house, and test Me now in this," says the Lord of hosts, "if I will not open for you the windows of heaven and pour out for you a blessing until it overflows."

4. Giving Acknowledges That God Owns it All

If we are truly surrendered to God then everything we have is His. After all, what do we have, that hasn't been given to us?

God is the owner of all that we have and we are merely the stewards of it. That's where tithing comes in. Giving Him the first 10 percent says "God, this is just giving You back what's already Yours. Thank You for the other 90 percent you let me keep." What a good and generous God!

Having the steward mentality reminds us that He owns it all, our bodies, our homes, our money, our children, our jobs, our possessions. As the saying goes: He's either Lord of all, or He isn't Lord at all.

To tithe is literally to give a tenth of one's income. Although some believe that's Old Testament Law (to give a whole tenth of what one makes), Jesus taught, in the New Testament to give our all. Personally, my husband and I have always seen a tithe (10 percent) as a great guideline or starting point in giving to the Lord. The tenth is the minimum God once required.

Today, why can't I give my tithe (a tenth) and my offerings (anything I can give above the tenth)? Sound radical? That's the kind of discipleship Jesus taught.

When we radically give, we are radically blessed.

5. Giving Leads to Joy

In 2 Corinthians 9:7, we read: "Each of you should give what you have decided in your heart to give, not reluctantly or under compulsion, for God loves a cheerful giver." The Greek word for cheerful is hilaro, where we get our English word hilarious. Although many pastors teach that verse is saying we are to give hilariously (and who really does that?) the word hilaro in its original context to its original audience meant "joyful, cheerful, non-reluctant, already inclined, won over."

In other words, give preparedly and with an anticipation of what God will do to multiply it for His purposes. That kind of giving produces joy, and an excitement of wanting to give more. That's another biblical reason to give money away, even if we don't think we have enough.

6.Giving Blesses Us—Abundantly

Do you realize the more you give, the more God will give you…so that you can continue to give? That's right. We don't give because then we'll get. We give out of gratitude for what God has given to us, and so that God will give us more so we can give more. That's the essence of giving in the New Testament.

Jesus said, "Give, and you will receive. Your gift will return to you in full—pressed down, shaken together to make room for more, running over, and poured into your lap. The amount you give will determine the amount you get back" (Luke 6:38, NLT).

Furthermore, 2 Corinthians 9:6 says, "Whoever sows sparingly will also reap sparingly, and whoever sows generously will also reap generously." Verse 8 adds: "And God is able to bless you abundantly so that in all things at all times, having all that you need, you will abound in every good work" (emphasis added).

That is a promise of abundance to those who abundantly give.

7. Giving Makes Us More Compassionate and Involved in God's Work

A few years into our marriage, my husband was no longer satisfied with what he called passive giving. "It's too easy to just drop a check in the offering plate when it passes by and expect someone else to put that money to work for God's kingdom," he said. "Let's be actively involved in what God's doing." We started praying about where and to whom God wanted us to give and then putting money directly into the hands of those whom God placed on our hearts.

That required prayer, waiting upon Him, looking around for where He might be working, and being attentive to listen. Thus began our adventure in active giving.

To this day, we find more joy, blessing, and evidence of God's divine work when we ask Him to open our eyes to the needs around us. In addition to giving to our local church—which can then put money into the hands of people it ministers to—and in addition to sending money overseas for a child in Indonesia to eat and be educated, we ask God to show us monthly who in our sphere of influence or among the body of Christ needs affirmation that God is supplying their every need.

More times than not, He's put someone in our path who just lost a job, just lost a house, just had a baby, just started coming to church, or just prayed for a miracle. We've found it is not just cheerful but hilarious to be one of the vessels through which God provides and meets a need in another believer's life.

Go ahead. Trust Him what He's given you. Step out, actively give, do it cheerfully and experience far more joy than you had when you kept it all to yourself.

10 Reasons Why 'It Is More Blessed to Give Than to Receive'

The most unbelieved beatitude in the Bible is: "It is more blessed to give than receive" (Acts 20:35). These words, quoted by Paul, as well known are not found in any one of the four Gospels, but are nonetheless genuine. They only preserve a fragment of the sayings and doings of our Lord (John 21:25). Giving, even here, secures more real happiness than receiving, and besides, is Godlike and blesses forever. (People's New Testament)

The giver happier than the getter? Surely some mistake? That goes against all our intuitions and instincts. So let me help you to believe it and act upon it by giving you ten reasons why it is more blessed to give than to receive.

What Did Jesus Mean When He Said 'More Blessed to Give Than Receive'?

The Tony Evans Bible Commentary tells us, "Indeed, in God's economy you will be more blessed if you're a spiritual conduit rather than a spiritual cul-de-sac. God wants to work through you so that you will be a blessing to others. If you have the capacity to address a need (with your money, your time, or your encouragement), be used by God to give to and meet that need. God will return the favor."

When we give, we are putting ourselves in a place of humility and offering that God shows favor upon. God is looking to bless those who obey Him and pursue the things of His kingdom on earth! Now let's take a specific look at 10 reasons why it is more blessed to give than receive.

1. Giving Obeys God's Command

The Old Testament has way more commands about financial giving – who, when, and how much – than the New Testament. Maybe the New Testament writers just assumed that as God had given far more to us in the New Testament – giving Himself to death – that our giving should follow fairly logically and easily. But, just in case we might miss the link, there are clear New Testament commands also (e.g. 1 Corinthians 1:2). As all of God's commands are given to enhance our lives, obeying this command will increase our happiness.

2. Giving Submits to God's Lordship

Every act of obedience recognizes that there is a higher authority in our lives, that there is a Lord over us who is entitled to honor and respect. Due to our temperament, personality, or circumstances, we may find some commands relatively easy to obey. Our submission is really tested in the areas where our own nature and situation make obedience more difficult. For most of us, money is one of those areas. Our wallet is often the last citadel to fall to God's rule, and even when it does fall, it gets rebuilt and re-secured again all too quickly. If only we could remember that Divine Lordship is not a threat; rather it's the place of greatest safety.

3. Giving Exhibits God's Heart

God is THE giver of every good and perfect gift (James 1:17). As His image-bearers, we are called to copy His giving, to be mini-pictures of His infinitely large heart. The larger our hearts (and the wider our hands), the larger the picture we paint of God's character. What do people think of God when they think of the way you use your money?

4. Giving Illustrates God's Salvation

At the heart of the Gospel is sacrificial self-giving (John 3:16). That's why when the Apostle Paul wanted to encourage the Corinthians to give more, he pointed them to the person and work of Christ. "For you know the grace of our Lord Jesus Christ, that though He was rich, yet for your sakes He became poor, that you through His poverty might become rich" (2 Corinthians 2:9). Yes, you abound in faith, love, etc., but "see that you abound in this grace also." When we give sacrificially, painfully, for the benefit of others, we are faintly and on a small scale preaching the Gospel message.

5. Giving Trusts God's Provision

The biggest deterrent to giving is fear, the fear that if I give away too much, I won't have enough for this or that. When we give sacrificially, above and beyond what is comfortable and easy, we are expressing our faith and trust in God to provide for us and our family. This is not an argument for folly but for faith. Many Christians have discovered the joy of casting their crumbs of bread upon the waters and multiple loaves returning after many days (Ecclesiastes 11:1). It's such a joy to see God fulfill His promise of provision when we obey Him.

6. Giving Widens God's Smile

The Lord loves a cheerful giver (2 Corinthians 2:7). It delights Him to see His people gladly opening their hearts and hands to provide for the needs of His Church and indeed of all His creatures. Through Paul, God repeatedly commends and praises those who gave of their funds and of themselves to Gospel work (2 Corinthians 8:1). There's nothing that makes a Christian happier than knowing that she's made God happy, and happy giving means a happy God.

7. Giving Advances God's Kingdom

Many of us have contributed to Apple in one way or another. We have helped to grow the company from a garage operation to the worldwide empire it is today. And I'm happy about that, as it's a company that has brought many blessings to the world. But think of what blessing results when we fund the mission of Christ's church. We are paying salaries of ministers and missionaries. We are funding resources for outreach, evangelism, and discipleship. But above all, we are investing in the spiritual and eternal welfare of people from every nation, tribe, kindred, and tongue. Our dollars are changing homes, relationships, countries, and even the eternal destiny of many souls.

8. Giving Promotes God's Sanctification

Giving not only promotes God's work through us, but also God's work in us, our sanctification. Giving money, especially when it pains us, requires much self-denial and self-crucifixion. However, as every act of giving weakens and even breaks our sinful and selfish nature, the more God's grace spreads in our hearts. Yes, money leaves our pockets, but sin also leaves our hearts. And that's a great deal. Priceless actually.

9. Giving Testifies to God's Power

Although we are not to let our left hand know what our right hand does, it's pretty obvious that Christians give a lot to their churches and Christian charities. Even secular observers have noticed with amazement how generous Christians often are with their money. They may not say it, but they surely must think it: "This must be the real deal for people to give away so much of their own money. They must really believe this stuff. The God they worship and serve must be incredibly powerful to make people so generous."

10. Giving Praises God's Character

Giving in a right spirit is an act of worship. It is rendering Him a tribute of praise. It is saying. "You gave me everything and here is a small expression of my gratitude and praise for all your good gifts. It's only a token, a sample of what I really feel, but you know the heart that lies behind it. As David sang: "What shall I render to the Lord for all his benefits towards me?" (Psalms 116:12).

Do you now see how giving makes us more blessed than getting? We can get so much happiness when we see how God is glorified in our giving and when we see Him bless others through our giving.

The Four Types Of Giving According To The Bible

Did you know that there are four types of giving as written in the Bible? You must know all of these. If you understand the differences of each, then you will see how these acts can reward you in life.

Here are the four types of giving according to the Bible:

1. Tithes

Tithes often get confused with offerings, but both are very different from each other.

According to the Bible, tithes are 10% of your income (Leviticus 27:30), and it can't count as an offering. Anything you give more than the required tithe is what counts as an offering.

Remember that the land and all its fruits were given by God. It's our way of recognizing Him as the provider of all things.

But tithes are more than an act of recognition. It's also a way of giving thanks for all the blessings that you are receiving. All your income came from God. So, you can think of the tithe as a way of giving back in gratitude for what we received.

Tithing was mentioned in the Bible a couple of times. But the first act of tithing was done by Abraham. He just came from battle and was met by the Priest/King Melchizedek who attributed his victory to God and blessed him for it. Then Abraham gave him a tenth of everything (Genesis 14:19-20).

Though tithing was commanded in the Old Testament, the New Testament tells us that we should not neglect the weightier issues. Yes, it's good to offer a portion of our income to God but we should not forget to offer justice, mercy, and faithfulness (Matthew 23:23). These should go hand in hand. We can't practice one while neglecting the other.

2. The Seed or Offerings

As mentioned, offerings differ from tithes. Unlike tithing, which has a required amount of how much you should give, offerings are more of a free will. It's up to you how much seed you want to give.

Although the more you give, the more you will receive (Luke 6:38). Think of it as the more seeds you sow, the more plants you can harvest.

So where should you give your offerings or plant your seed? The Bible says that the source of your spiritual food should receive your offerings (1 Corinthians 9:11).

3. The First Fruits

The first fruits are usually done once a year or for every new blessing that you receive (Deuteronomy 14:22).

For example, the house of God should receive the full amount of your first salary that you get from your new job. An increase in your salary should also be given to your spiritual storehouse.

Any new blessings that you receive count as a first fruit, so all these should be offered to God (Proverbs 3:9).

Giving your first fruits once a year will show how grateful you are for the blessings that you received from Him.

4. Alms-giving

Unlike those three types of giving above which you should give to God, alms are for humankind. Your compassion and sympathy will lead you to help the less fortunate and the needy.

There are many ways on how you can give alms. There are lots of soup kitchens out there that help the less fortunate where you can donate food, clothes, and even some cash.

Although most people do alms-giving, many do it the wrong way.

In the Bible, it says that you should give alms in secret so you can protect the dignity of those who are in crisis. Many are helping others but are bragging about it as well.

All of us can help the needy, but only a few can help others with the purest of intentions.

When you practice all these types of giving, then you can have your financial life under control. But remember, you need to have the right intentions and motivations when giving.

Your heart should be pure when doing such selfless acts and God will bestow more blessings upon you.

11 BIBLE GIVERS

1.The Spontaneous Giver can be seen in the young boy with his fishes and loaves (John 6:9). I do not think this young man woke up that day committed to giving away all he had. However, when the surprise opportunity arose, he held loosely to his stuff. Jesus then took his meager portions and blessed thousands. Live with an open hand seeking much fruit.

2. The Devoted Giver can be seen in Cornelius (Acts 10:2). The Bible says that he was devout, prayerful, and generous. He lived this way both privately and publicly. It was how he led his family and also how he led his career (see Acts 10:7). In this passage we learn that his consistent devotion was recognized by God, and he was honored with a greater assignment.

3.The Faith-Filled Giver can be seen in the widow and her offering (Luke 21:2). This passage really interested me because of its level of description. This poor widow gave two small copper coins. Her gift just keeps getting smaller and smaller the more words the author uses. However, her result, as stated by Jesus, was that she gave more than everyone else because she gave all she had to live on. Evidently Jesus does measure the faith amount. He makes small things big.

4.The Creative Giver can be seen in Barnabas (Acts 4:36-37). Barnabas had something valuable, a piece of property he owned. However, his eternal perspective and the needs around him caused a generous response. The property he owned was actually a gift from God to meet the needs of another. He sold the property and brought 100% of the proceeds to the apostles so they could meet the needs of the community. Ananias and Sapphira pretended to do the same in Acts 5. I love how these two stories are found back to back in the Bible.

5.The Crazy Giver can be seen in the lady with her alabaster jar of perfume (Mark 14:3). This extremely generous gift was given directly to and benefitting Jesus. The Bible tells us that this perfume was worth more than an entire year's wage! It was such a crazy-big gift that it shocked those who were present. They actually rebuked her for being wasteful. Instead Jesus applauds her. He says it is a clear reminder of how generous the gospel really is.

6.Unsuspecting Giver – The book of Luke tells us about some of the early actions of the 12 disciples and several ladies (Luke 8:1-3). These early recruits were newbies in the faith, straight out of the marketplace. On top of that, the women are described as formerly having evil spirits, diseases, and demons. This is probably not the list that most would make heroes of or at least not just yet. Still these early adopters who are taking their first steps of faith are said to be supporting Jesus "out of their own means" and Jesus wants to make sure you know them. There are no high and lofty requirements to generosity, just give.

7.Called Giver – Luke also introduces us to an extreme giving request of Jesus (Luke 9:3 and 10:4). He called his early disciples, over 80 of them, to give up everything for the sake of a short-term mission trip. He sent them all out into the harvest, to share the good news and help people with their needs. Jesus called them to go, take nothing, not a dime or a change of clothes, not even a snack. We are called to support Jesus both out of our means and at times by giving up all we have. Don't worry, you won't be the first or last person Jesus asks or sends out. Just one of many who have learned to enjoy the adventure.

8.Compassionate Giver – Luke 10:35 introduces us to a fictional character, but the story is powerfully real. Today we call him The Good Samaritan. A man who allowed his day to be interrupted. He didn't permit the inconvenience or expense to stop him. Whatever others may say about his investment in a troubled person did not matter. He gave compassionately and comprehensively. No trite pat on the back here. Rather he gave time, energy, and resources over an extended period for a guy he may never see again. Giving people are both simple and alert. This story could look a little heroic, but it's really just common courtesy. If you can't be stopped in your tracks, you will never be able to give compassionately.

9.Investing Giver – Luke 10:15 is another fictional character in a very real situation. It's a successful business man tempted by greed. His thriving business has put him in a quandary. His barns are too small, so he builds bigger barns to store his wealth and coast into the future. Only life changes, and his money can't solve his spiritual problem. Focusing on an earthly investment did not pay off as he anticipated. Jesus' instructions are to live by faith, and don't trust in worldly wealth. Instead, sell your possessions and give to the poor. This will reap an unstoppable reward, and grow a heart towards God. Seeing the future clearly helps us hold loosely to the things of today.

10.Fake Giver – Luke 18:22 shares about a man who lived on the dark side of generosity. We commonly call him the Rich Young Ruler. He appears to desire a relationship with Jesus, however as the story unfolds we learn where his heart really is. He is so proud of his religious life, then Jesus exposes that it is paper thin. No hero here. Only a stark reminder that the Rich Young Ruler can be a stealthy resident in the life of very religious people. He chooses to fail at generosity, and he had all the resources to accomplish it. How sad.

11.Transformed Giver – Luke 19:8 provides us with an immediate and rather bold response of faith. It comes from Zacchaeus. He is brand new in Jesus' way, like less than one day. He is really wealthy just like the Investing Giver and the Fake Giver. Jesus doesn't ask him to show his faith through generosity at all. Nope, still this doesn't stop Zaccheus from thinking about it on his own. He confesses his financial sins, having been a cheat and thief. Then he demonstrates a changed life by giving half his possessions to the poor and paying back anyone he wronged 4x what he owed them. Jesus said we would be known by things like love and fruit. Generosity is a great demonstration if both.

The Importance of Giving

One of the biggest questions that philosophers, psychologists, and other scientific thinkers have been reflecting on is the question of doing good–altruism.

What Does It Mean to Be Altruistic?

Usually, it is defined as "self-sacrifice" or "giving to others regardless of the personal consequences". Giving can take many forms, especially among humans: we give gifts, our time, resources, support, emotions, etc.

But what if we do good things for others knowing that we'll reap some benefits for ourselves? Is that still altruism? This is what many researchers and thinkers have been debating over for centuries now. Does a selfless altruistic act even exist? Or is it always motivated by personal gains?

If we view altruism as laughter, we can say that we often laugh to make other people feel good, but we also do it because we enjoy laughing, or because we have an interest in the other person liking us. It's difficult to untangle these motivations.

Similar to laughter, acts of kindness mean a lot to other people, but to us, too. Selfless giving is considered a high virtue, but this very consideration is what makes its altruism questionable: Are we doing it for the sake of being awarded as virtuous, or because we truly want to give?

And while these are great questions for exercising our thought processes and introspecting our motivation, we can also ask ourselves:

Are the answers ultimately important?

Or is the result more important: us feeling well, meaningful, connected to the people around us, and others feeling noticed, taken care of, and important?

It's on each one of us to answer these questions. In the meantime, we'll list some of the most important aspects and consequences of giving.

Giving Supports Our Health

There are many studies, especially since the rise of positive psychology that consider the relationship between kindness, positivity, giving, and other similar positive practices and human health.

PHYSICAL HEALTH AND GIVING

Did you know that kind, giving people tend to live longer and healthier lives? They report fewer symptoms of pain and aches. Studies have shown that volunteering is more important in lowering your likelihood of dying than exercising four times a week–almost as important as quitting smoking.

In his book, Why Good Things Happen to Good People, preventative medicine professor Stephen Post reported that giving to others can increase the immune system response among people with a chronic illness.

MENTAL HEALTH AND GIVING

Acts of giving and kindness also play a preventative role when it comes to our mental health. Such acts stimulate the reward (dopamine and endorphin) in brain areas and thus make us feel good and positive. This makes an impact on our cognition, emotions, and psyche, and increases our perceived self-value, confidence, and self-worth. This way we prevent ourselves from falling victim to depression, anxiety, and other mental health issues.

How is this possible? Why is the act of giving so beneficial for our overall physical wellbeing?

The most probable hypothesis is that volunteering, kindness to others, giving, and other altruistic acts lower our perceived stress and the intensity of our stress response. This way, instead of excreting "bad" neurotransmitters and hormones like cortisol and adrenaline that alert our organism and harm our health, we are much more in balance with our entire being.

Helping others makes us feel good, and we can feel it both physically and mentally: people reported feeling more energetic, less depressed, and more self-worthy. It's like helping others has the potential to trigger euphoria.

Giving Makes Us Happy

Besides giving us energy and making us more energetic and healthy, giving ultimately makes us happy. We've mentioned already how volunteer work and kindness can lower symptoms of depression and make us "high" on dopamine and endorphins.

This all means that giving is a much more important element of happiness than receiving.

Being able to give makes us feel like we're making a big impact on someone's life, encouraging us to do more good and uncover a different perspective of happiness. In support, studies detect a clear correlation between volunteering and happiness. Teenagers who are motivated to help others feel much happier, more excited, engaged, involved, and active compared to their peers who are not motivated by altruism. They are also more socially intelligent and confident.

Giving Promotes Positive Values

Giving inspires further giving. This is just one of the many positive values that the act of giving instills. Apart from feeling grateful for being important to someone, the receivers very often also become inspired and wish to become givers themselves.

Furthermore, if you give to others, you are more likely to be rewarded, and receive something in return, either from the same person or someone else. Such exchanges represent the base for other positive emotions and values, such as trust, cooperation, intimacy, and life satisfaction. Giving also strengthens positive relationships and collaboration not only between two individuals, but within a social community as well.

Buildings or neighborhoods in which all neighbors know each other, have mutual community activities, and help each other (helping the elderly, watching each other's children, exchanging/borrowing things, etc.) tend to have less crime, disputes, and be more satisfied in life.

Giving and Gratitude

It's quite unexpected how giving evokes gratitude on both ends: both the giver and the receiver can feel grateful in the act. The giver might be expressing their gratitude for something, and at the same time make the receiver feel grateful as well.

So far, research has revealed that gratitude plays an important part in our happiness, health, social relationships, and overall wellbeing. It's another mediator to perceived stress that makes us more resilient and optimistic when life gets hard.

By giving to others, you pass the beautiful feeling of gratitude on. Once you feel grateful for what you have now, or what you have received, you'll most likely wish to spread appreciation and joy around.

How important is giving to you? Are you a giver or a receiver? Do you notice that you receive more when you feel and act in a giving way? Do you think that's a coincidence or is there an explanation?

There are so many things to be gifted: objects, love, patience, attention, time, advice, forgiveness, presence. A gift is the most beautiful way to thank someone, apologize, show how we feel, or make friends with someone.

Giving is an act of art because it sums up the most beautiful wishes, feelings, and messages. From a small act of kindness like a smile to bigger deeds like supporting a dear friend or helping a team member achieve something that's important to them—it's an art. Ultimately, it helps you become a better and happier person

Spread the love!

9 798848 480252